This is
not
---
my
cat

This is not my cat

Feline friends who picked their humans

Stevie Holcomb

Smith Street Books

Contents

Introduction 8

Clyde 86

Misty 88

Malcolm 90

New Friend 92

Handyman 94

Pablo 96

Eusebio 98

Fern 100

Franklin 102

Bella 104

Dinner Guest 106

Lockdown Buddy 108

Introduction

It's happened to me, several times – a random cat shows up and decides that we are now friends. The first was a fluffy orange tabby that hung around the community theater where I was directing *Barefoot in the Park*. We called him Knichi – the dish of eel and who knows what else that Mr. Velasco makes in the show. Knichi certainly had another name, another home, but he was the theater cat – for that show, anyway – stopping by after rehearsal for a head skritch or two before he would go on his merry way.

Knichi wasn't seen before, or after, but there's been other theater cats. When we were rehearsing *The Full Monty*, my friend Kelly and I would keep our eyes peeled on the way home for the two tabbies – one grey and one orange – whom we named Monty and Rocky. We weren't sure if they were street cats or had homes, but they cheered us up every time we saw them.

Knichi, Monty, and Rocky aren't alone, though – they have friends. All over the internet, I noticed stories about cats showing up in people's lives – in their homes, their cars, their work – unexpectedly and delightfully. They'd wander in through open doors, doggie doors, car doors … They'd show up on patios during cookouts or on neighborhood strolls. People would be amazed to discover that pregnant momma cats had chosen their homes to give birth in.

So, I started the Facebook group *My House, Not My Cat*, for the wide community of cat adoptees. Eventually, we grew enough that I couldn't handle the group alone – I added Janet and Lex to the team, and two years later, Julia, Aly, Morgan, and Leah. I can't thank them enough for their assistance, love, and for the friendship that we have built over the years.

We have seen so many stories, it was hard to choose for this book, but I have pulled together some of our best. Thank you to each and every person who sent in their own Knichis or Montys. I'm normally just a humble person in Virginia who sells houses and volunteers in community theater – but we are all connected by these visiting fluff balls: our Not My Cats. Some have names we've given them, some are neighbor cats that choose to spend part of their day with us, but they all bring a bit of sunshine into our lives. We hope they do to yours, too.

– STEVIE

Stinky Stripey

Stinky Stripey – named as such due to the stripes in his fur and his overall scruffy stinkiness. He is not a stray, but a well-cared-for cat who simply loves to roll around in dry mud and dirt.

I have learned from my mistakes: the times I left the doors open for a few seconds, only to find the little creeper in my house. Trying to remove him is challenging – from under furniture, he attacks! He voices his loud disapproval when he is removed from the premises.

FRAUD

THIS IS NOT MY CAT

He has also been found committing fraud a few (very long) roads away from us. A friend of a neighbor mentioned a cat that they call the "Fluffy bastard." They shared a photo, and we made a positive identification of Stinky Stripey.

It turns out, he has very similar features to their cat. He had taken advantage of this likeness by posing as said cat and finishing her food most days, while she looked on in shock.

Stinky Stripey is an opportunist, and no jurisdiction is safe from his traveling crime.

– EMILY

Dill Pickle Soup

This sweet baby showed up one night, starving and cold, while we were searching for our missing kitten. We weren't supposed to keep him, but he never left and Pickle's now a heckin' chonk living his best life. He loves taking naps (which we are not allowed to talk during!) and hanging out with his best friend Kiwi, our dog. We weren't supposed to keep Dill Pickle Soup, but he was never claimed (I guess he claimed us), and we fell in love!

– ASHLEY

Ted

THIS IS NOT MY CAT

This is my glass of water. This is my
house. But this is not my cat drinking
my water. It's my neighbor's cat Ted,
who doesn't have great manners.

This is my bathroom. This is my bath.
This is Ted who is still not my cat.

– ANNE

"This is Randall

He lives down our road in a very nice house but prefers to hang out in our sink."

– BARBARA

Toby

THIS IS NOT MY CAT

The cat on the left is mine. His buddy on the right is not. His name is Toby and he belongs to the next-door neighbors, but he visits us at least once a day to hang out with our four kitties, grab a snack, and have a little drink. My husband even cut a little kitty door into our fence. His owners help watch my three indoor kitties when we're out of town, and I (and most of our street) watch out for the Tobbers.

- PATRICIA

I'd asked my boyfriend for a while if we could get an orange creamsicle cat. We were always planning to wait until we move into a larger house, but one night, this little guy walked right up to us and begged to be pet. I took him inside for the night, since it was getting chilly, and he promptly made himself far too comfortable.

We took him to the Humane Society on my birthday, where we found out that his previous adopter had been blacklisted. Fast-forward to today, Mushroom is a spoiled housecat with a BIG personality! He is loud and spirited, and he always wants to be right in the middle of the action. He begs to be held, plays with any small object he can get his paws on, constantly wants to go outside on his leash, and loves to sleep on my head.

I couldn't have asked for a better birthday gift!

- MORGAN

Freeloader

Once upon a time, Freeloader would come in through the cat flap and eat my cat's food.

I didn't see him for a few months, but fast-forward to me finding Freeloader loafing around inside. He wouldn't let me approach and gave me a sound meoooooow when I looked at him, quickly disappearing behind the furnace.

When he first appeared, Freeloader didn't have a collar. But now, he has a cute little one with a bell, so he is possibly an escape artist who occasionally feels like I warrant a visit.

- ANDREA

Sassy

I used to affectionately call this guy my "porch gremlin." He showed up at my house in November – I took a nap during a bad windstorm, and when I woke up and looked outside, I saw this fuzzbutt.

He originally wanted nothing to do with me. He'd sneak into my yard, and as soon as he saw me, he'd run. He'd go without visiting for weeks at a time, so it was a surprise whenever I saw him, but I'd often look for him and make sure he was okay.

I strove to gain his trust. And I slowly did.

Fast-forward to the end of February, I injured my arm and had to go on medical leave for about four months. Before this, he'd only come at night or early morning when it was dark. Suddenly, he showed up every afternoon. I'd sit with him outside on a chair or safely on the steps where I could get up without having to use my bad arm.

Every day, I'd work on gaining his trust and by mid-spring, I was able to pet him. By the time summer came around, I would open the door and he would waltz inside for food and love ... and then promptly leave when he'd had enough of both.

He's a big reason I'd get out of bed and get off the couch. He helped me emotionally heal while I medically healed, and he comes now when I call for him and lets me pet his fuzzy kitty belly.
Now, we call him Sassy.

– EVIE

THIS IS NOT MY CAT

Matilda

This is Matilda, who visits at least three other houses. She usually meets me after work for treats and then goes. Tonight, she's decided to stay, probably because a) it's raining, b) she's sensed I'm heading off for a holiday soon, and c) I want to go to bed, and she knows I won't make her leave. Always the way ... lucky I'm a patient gal who loves her visits.

- CATHY

"This goth girl seemed like she was sneering at me. Gave her food and she went away happy. She has a home, of course – she's even bigger than my own cat! But who could resist that sneer?"

– ALEAH

Goth
Girl

Reginald

For a week or so, my cat Artemis was acting weird, not allowing me to close the window at night. If I did, he wouldn't let me sleep, trying to break everything. Okay Artemis: window stays open at night. But I also noticed that he was eating a lot and making a mess.

Well, now I know why. At 5:45am, I woke up to find Reginald, a cat who visits us every night, inside. On the couch. I think he'd been sleeping inside the whole week, which is why Artemis wouldn't let me close the window: because Reginald had been sleeping over. Turns out, when Reginald popped by earlier every night, he was coming to see if it was time for bed.

He's suspicious of everyone, but these days, he's friendlier and plays with Artemis. I leave blankets on the couch for him, and my dad is planning on adopting him once we gain his trust. On the bad side, I do have a minor cold because I've been sleeping with the window wide open, but I don't care as long as Reginald is safe and warm! I can always get another blanket for myself, but Reginald might not have another warm place to spend the night.

- PAULA

One day last August, Harry showed up at our house and shoved his way in as I was opening the door. I hadn't planned on another indoor cat because my 16-year-old cat Tabi required so much care. But when I took Harry to the vet, they told me he was an abandoned senior cat and likely wouldn't last long on his own – he wasn't grooming and needed to eat. Thus, Harry became an indoor cat.

Tabi and Harry really got along. I think Tabi grooming Harry helped kickstart Harry to self-groom again. And Harry would calm Tabi instantly with licks during Tabi's chronic senile crying moments – I nearly cried the first time I saw how quickly Harry calmed Tabi. I am so grateful Harry was here to help me deal with Tabi's passing in the early days of 2020. He adopted us at exactly the right time, and I love him so much.

- ANDREA

Harry

Local Bully

This boy lives two doors down but has bullied us into letting him into our house 24/7.

When I moved last year, I thought he was a feral cat. I would leave food out for him until, one day, I walked in to the bathroom, and he was just sitting in it, staring at me.

That was just the beginning – he started to follow me everywhere: the pub at 10pm. All the way to the park, where he would hang out with me until we walked back.

His owners want him to stop coming over, but he will not leave. He sits in the front window, like he's trying to tell them to mind their own business.

When we tried to take him home, he flipped out – he will not go in their house. He just runs back and sits on our doorstep where he scratches the door until we let him in. Our neighbors are mad, but I can't ignore this cat who would rather sit in the rain and meow at my door than go back to their house.

I love him more than life and I don't know what to do.

- SHERI

Leroy

I came downstairs from my office
to get a drink and this handsome boy
was inside my dining room, looking out
on to my deck. How did he get here?!
How long has he been here?!?
Did I forget getting a fourth cat?

He let me pet him while he chirped and
even let me pick him up and carry him
around. Turns out, this boy's name is
Leroy, and he lives a block over where
he's now back with his family.

- DANIELLE

"My garden,
not my cat.

She belongs to a
neighbor and visits
me when I get
lonely working
from home."

– CHARLOTTE

Felix

My neighbor's cat is obsessed with my cats, dogs, and daughter. (He's less polite to my cats, but he sure decided their toys are alright.)

But today took the cake. The front door was closed because it rained, so Felix took a scary journey to see where his friends were.

- MICHELLE

Feline Stalker

Even though this cat is not my cat, she finds ways to punish me when I go away for any duration. Namely – sitting on my decking waiting for me, and then turning her back. Weirdly, this only makes me want to please her more. I'm in a toxic relationship with a cat that is not my cat.

There is almost nowhere in the house I can go where she does not stare in and meow plaintively. Except the bedroom. (If her face appears there, then she has learned to levitate.) It's making working from home quite hard.

Is she my new pet? Or a feline stalker?

- ELIZABETH

A conversation between my boyfriend and I:

"What's the butter in the fridge with
'Brown Cat' written on it?"

"That's Brown Cat's lick butter."

"We're gonna have to throw that away."

"No we're not, let him live his life."

(You might not be mine, Brown Cat,
but I got your back.)

- MORGAN

Brown
Cat

Rory

Four years ago, we brought Joey home to live with us. But after a few months, we became aware that we had another cat in the yard. At first, nothing much: Joey's food bowls were cleaned out, and I once saw the end of a thin brown tail disappearing through the cat flap.

Eventually, the visitor gained confidence, and the two cats became firm friends, sleeping a couple of feet apart, chasing each other around the house at night.

Turns out, our visitor was a neighbor named Rory, but the next January, his owners moved away. That was the last we saw of him for over a year, until he climbed in through a high window. We found out that his owners had moved about half a mile away, over woods and fields, along the river. He's been a regular visitor since, but we have always had to call his owners to retrieve him, as his Cat-Nav only works in one direction.

At the moment, Rory is with us for a month, while his staff is in India. Joey and Rory are taking turns going out in the pouring rain, to get towel dried again: reunited best friends.

- DAVID

Mamas

THIS IS NOT MY CAT

One night, I had Mom over to my place. Around 7:30 or 8pm, she went outside, and then started rapidly beating on the living room window, telling me to come outside because there were, not one, but FOUR cats on the porch.

Over the next three weeks, one of them stuck around. I worked on gaining her trust, and she started coming around daily, greeting us at the door when she heard our cars out front. I would call out "Mamas," and she would come RUNNING no matter where she was at – she could have been two streets over, but she'd come.

My fiancé and I decided to catch Mamas, get her vetted, and find her a home because she wasn't going to survive out there. Of course, the last part of the plan hasn't happened: she's worked her way into our hearts and is probably going to become our new cat. Mamas is great with our puppy, cats, and daughter: one of the sweetest kitties ever. We don't understand how someone could just kick her out, but we're glad she came into our lives and chose us.

- BRITTANY

Cleo

"This girl showed up and just made herself at home. She really is the sweetest thing and she's now named Cleo.

I now have five cats.

They just keep showing up here?"

– KATHLEEN

Pickle

Pickle started showing up out of nowhere at our flat. We were happy to let her in and she was happy to hang out like she owned the place.

One afternoon, a few months after she first appeared, she came bounding in with a sponge in her mouth. We still have no idea where she got it, but she was very proud of herself as she presented us with her gift.

Over the next year, we gifted her various sponges, which she promptly destroyed (after cuddling them).

We ended up meeting Pickle's owners (our next-door neighbors), who informed us that Pickle's actual name is Jaffa. I never got around to asking if they were able to keep sponges out at home ...

- JENNIE

Sony

Sony, otherwise known as Tony, is a neighborhood cat and long-time resident of my share house. He was a constant visitor before any of us moved in, and continues to frequent our porch, backyard, couches, and beds. We've never fed him (aside from the time we were afraid he was dying and bought him a fillet of salmon), but he still spends at least 90% of the day in or around the house.

The tap in the bathroom used to leak, which may have been his original pull to the house - flowing fresh water. These days, his water is provided in a bowl which he can drink from in between taking naps on top of us, or on our beds when we aren't home (we do let him out if the house is empty).

A very large and grumpy man, he is also extremely sweet and will happily let you carry him around and pet him while he drools all over you. He has left us many dead animals in his time - a gesture we appreciate in spirit, though less in delivery. If spotted out on the street, he always gives us the cold shoulder: a busy man about town. An hour later, though, he will turn up to sleep in one of his many favorite spots. And if you don't see him when you get home, you can always call his name and he'll likely come running (or appear at the back porch where he'll stare in until the door opens).

Eventually, we will all move while Sony continues to preside over his domain. But he will forever live in our hearts (and on my housemates' legs, where they got matching tattoos of Tony): the true cat of our hearts, if not our legal possession.

- **TENZIN**

Cinnamon

THIS IS NOT MY CAT

We saw an orange blob on the house camera eating from the feral cat bowl. I posted on the neighborhood app, asking if he was someone's. Two weeks later, I finally found his owner.

But Sam just would not stop hanging around our house, day in and day out. He would get in my car, or he would lay on our doormat, to be sure to not miss our arrivals. There were many days he could be spotted on the doorbell camera sitting – staring.

I finally let him in, and we called him Cinnamon. And he loved his new home. LOVED. I called his owner and she said, "He chose you."

Sam, now Cinnamon, really blossomed, playing and sleeping with the other pets. Unfortunately, love couldn't save him, and he eventually passed away from natural causes. But before he passed on, we went through his bucket list: 1. Eat tuna, 2. Sit in sunny window on forbidden kitchen counter, and finally 3. Lay outside under the big tree where we brought him treats and bowls of ice water.

I still miss that freeloading fool.

- LISEANNE

Hector

This stray kitten was living in my bushes and eating my cat's food. I trapped her with a cat trap and brought her in.

She was very feisty, but after I made Hector into a burrito, she became the biggest love bug. She is still very shy and hisses at new things, but she's found a nice, loving home. We weren't going to keep her, but we fell in love.

What's one more?

- MONICA

Tony

THIS IS NOT MY CAT

We call our friend Tony. Occasionally, he
sleeps here ... on my side of the bed. His owners
call him Chief, but he prefers Tony. (I can tell.)

I wonder if they know he has a vacation home?

- MARYANN

"Was not my cat.

Came inside.

Is now my cat
Sash, AKA
Sausage."

– KAYLA

Sausage

One day, out of the blue, this gorgeous girl comes up on our porch and jumps in my nephew's lap, instantly falling in love with him. We looked for her owner, but nobody responded, and she now lives on our front porch. She's a little skittish, but she's so friendly and sweet – she just wants pets all day.

Pumpkin doesn't want to come into the house, or sleep on the bed we bought her. Instead, she sleeps on the chairs, but she'll be getting her very own heated cat house for the winter. She's a strange one, but we love her with all her quirks!

- BRIANNA

Pumpkin

Leo

My house. My sewing machine.
My PPE assembly line. My supervisor?
I don't think cats need masks, Leo,
but thanks for pointing out that our
back door was ajar ...

- ROBYN

Frank

This is our little spooky girl, Frank. She's the tiniest Manx tuxedo that came wandering into our yard about two years ago. She had no collar and wasn't chipped, so we were pretty sure she was a stray from the neighborhood.

So, one day I leave for work and pat her on the head as I walk to my car. She was sitting in her normal spot on our front porch. When I come home in the afternoon I find her IN THE HOUSE. She had gotten into our basement from a window and up into ductwork that had fallen through a register and into the house.

So, she broke in. Now she's an inside cat.

- TIFFANY

THIS IS NOT MY CAT

"Cheddar Boye from next door likes to hang out on the roof of my porch and watch me in my room like a creep."

– MAES

Buddy

After moving with my family as a kid, I woke up
one morning to Buddy in the kitchen. She came
right up to me, sniffed me, walked to every room
in the house, sniffed them as well, then stood
at the door waiting to be let out.

After this, Buddy came by every single day for snuggles and kisses and would walk down to the bus stop with my brother and me every morning.

She sometimes chilled with other people around the neighborhood – on the way to school one day, I saw her staring at me from inside another woman's house. She became known as the neighborhood cat, everybody feeding and petting her. But nonetheless, Buds chose my house, and my family. Suddenly, she wouldn't even leave our porch and garage. She stopped wandering the neighborhood, and stationed herself here with us.

It turns out, Buddy's owners abandoned her when they moved, so we brought this fluffy sweetheart inside.

I love my now senior sweetheart. She's about 15 years old and is the sweetest and most lovable cuddlebug you could ever ask for. She'll eat you out of house and home, then give you big Puss-in-Boots eyes to guilt trip you for even more. I'd give the world for her if I could: she is my world. My one of a kind! My Buddy!

- MAGNUS

Asper

Last year, new neighbors moved onto my parents' street, one of whom was extremely noisy (and nosy): Asper. A beautiful silver lady, she started appearing in the front yard. And the backyard. And the neighbors' yards. She loves a pet or a chat, meowing loudly while she tells you all about her day of breaking into people's properties and hearts.

My mom feeds her, which did not thrill the two cats my parents already owned – Asper became a frequent visitor to the back door. However, they

THIS IS NOT MY CAT

now know when the outdoor cat is fed, they are fed too. They have come to a resigned acceptance. Asper does not appear concerned, though, with them or the laws around breaking and entering. She terrified my younger brother when he heard noises coming from the downstairs storeroom one night, only to open the door to Asper. She had gotten in from under the house... somehow? She was rescued and returned outside, a bit dustier for her adventure.

She hasn't broken back in since, but she is always outside to say hello – a truly friendly neighbor.

- CONNOR

"My garage sale, not my cat...

do I just put a 'free' sticker on them?"

– KRISTAN

Clyde

This is Clyde. He actually belongs to the neighbors but hangs out at our house more than theirs. I have an Adult Foster Home and he has decided one of my residents belongs to him. He sits outside of her room and yowls at the door until she lets him in. He spends a lot of his nights there.

- SAMANTHA

THIS IS NOT MY CAT

Misty is our neighbor's cat. While she doesn't always appear during the day, during the night, there's a good chance that she will greet you on the street, meowing away. She likes to follow you inside, where she will give things a sniff and then carry on to the backyard – she mostly just uses our house as a hallway (and I guess us as doormen).

She'll pay us visits in the day, sometimes, hopping down from our roof into the backyard – if you hear a bell tinkling, that means Misty is here and ready for some pats. She's extremely friendly – we once saw her try to play with a dog on a walk, and if she's out and about at night and you pass her, she'll say hello and lead you back home. Whenever I'm in the yard, I always call her name in the hopes she'll come by and say hello. When she does decide to stay for a bit, she has a patch of grass she loves to sleep in, where she is always welcome.

– AVERY

THIS IS NOT MY CAT

This is our dog Ace's cat friend, Malcolm. Ace taught Malcolm how to use the doggie door.

Malcolm proceeded to let himself in whenever he felt like it. I have woken up with Malcolm sleeping at the foot of my bed. I have come home to no one there except Malcolm and Ace, partners in crime.

Eventually, we spoke with his owners, and they were more than happy for us to adopt him.

Now, he's moved in for good with his best friend Ace.

- BETH

New Friend

I saw this little cat right outside my window, watching the hummingbird feeder. I waggled a finger at her and she didn't flinch, so I opened the front door. She came over and allowed me to give her some pets and skritches. After a bit, she became curious and came inside.

She was very thin and obviously hungry, so I found a can of tuna and gave her a few bites, which she gobbled right up. After a second helping, she started exploring, checking each room. She stayed for a couple of hours before leaving.

She ended up eating a whole five-ounce can of tuna and about a cup of water. I'm hoping she'll come back again.

- PAUL

"Repair people were in my apartment. I went into my bedroom after they left and found this cat on my bed."

– STEVEN

Pablo

THIS IS NOT MY CAT

Pablo was adopted by my housemate Sonia after two of our cohorts in grad school heard a cat wailing in a storm drain and scooped up a noisy, half-drowned kitten.

The first year was difficult. He flung torn-up toilet paper everywhere, decided my head needed a bath at 3am, and managed to find previously undiscovered holes in our studio apartment. But I absolutely fell in love with Pablo. Since then, he has grown into a charming rascal who lolls about, looking as though he owns the place. His voice saved him from the storm drain and certainly hasn't failed him since. Even though Sonia and her partner trained him to sit like a gentleman before dinner, Pablo still lets everyone know that he's starving at least an hour beforehand. He's the most expressive cat I've ever met; I swear he communicates in full sentences, and can somehow tell everyone precisely how to become the best pillow.

Sadly, we're moving in a few months. I'm going to miss sitting at the window with Pabs, watching the street. For now, his next chapter will start with a few extra breakfast treats tomorrow.

- MEREDITH

Eusebio

My house. My neighbor's cat.

His name is Eusebio. And he feels
totally comfortable everywhere.

- ZEULA

THIS IS NOT MY CAT

Fern

I live on the third floor of an apartment building. One day, one of my roommates heard meowing at our back door and this sweetheart, Fern, bolted in. Thankfully her full name was on her collar, and we were able to return her to her rightful home. Our best guess is that her owner left their back door open and she somehow wandered to ours. She didn't visit for long, but Fern was super sweet and I miss her.

- LEAH

Franklin

This is the cat that we've been taking care of for years. He just started coming in the house. We built him a shelter, called him Franklin, and are occasionally able to pet him.

These days, Franklin has become picky about his food. My son thinks he's Six-Dinner Sid, but that hasn't stopped us from spending over $100 a month on food, for him and our cat Squeaky.

- TOBI

Bella

THIS IS NOT MY CAT

In our old house, a neighbor's cat started visiting. At first, she'd appear in the backyard. Then she let us pet her. Eventually, she started coming into the house where she'd be welcomed with food. She started coming over to hang out more and more, so we made her a cat door so that she could come in and out anytime she wanted.

We contacted her owners, who lived in a small apartment and didn't have time to give her much attention. In our house, there were plenty of housemates, and I was home to give her heaps and heaps of cuddles every day while she slept in my bed.

I had to say goodbye when we moved house, sadly, and I've never seen her again. These days, I always drive past our old house with rolled down windows and yell her name out the window, hoping she will appear.

- ALITTA

"I have three spoiled indoor cats. This is not one of them, but he usually comes by for dinner every evening."

– SUSAN

Lockdown Buddy

My flat, not my cat. This is one of the more confident neighborhood cats who visits every day without fail.

When I first moved in a year ago, she walked in like she owned the place and started meowing for attention. Now, she'll pop in for a snack, maybe hang around for pets or a nap, and then leave again. During the hard lockdown, she kept me company and brought me joy. I know she belongs to someone in the neighborhood because she's well fed, but she's so special to me.

- ROXANNE

Thanks

A huge thanks to everyone who contributed stories and photos of the cats in their lives. We couldn't have made this book without you and the cats who chose your laps to nap in.

Aleah	Elizabeth	Morgan S.
Alitta	Emily	Morgan P. S.
Andrea C.	Evie	Patricia
Andrea L.	Jennie	Paul
Anne	Kathleen	Paula
Ashley	Kayla	Robyn
Barbara	Kristan	Roxanne
Beth	Leah	Samantha
BriAnna	Liseanne	Sheri
Brittany	Maes	Steven
Cathy	Magnus	Susan
Charlotte	MaryAnn	Tenzin
Connor	Meredith	Tiffany
Danielle	Michelle	Tobi
David	Monica	Zeula

Published in 2022 by Smith Street Books
Naarm | Melbourne | Australia
smithstreetbooks.com

ISBN: 978-1-92275-403-5

Photographs © Respective cat adoptees
Cover photograph © Paul Hanaoka, Unsplash
Copyright text © Stevie Holcomb
Copyright design © Smith Street Books

Publisher: Paul McNally
Project editor: Avery Hayes
Design and layout: Madeleine Kane
Proofreader: Pam Dunne

Printed & bound in China by C&C Offset Printing Co., Ltd.

Book 228
10 9 8 7 6 5 4 3 2 1